Collins

Cherry Blossoms

General Awareness

LKG

FS2

SERIES EDITOR: RANI THIPPAVAZZULA

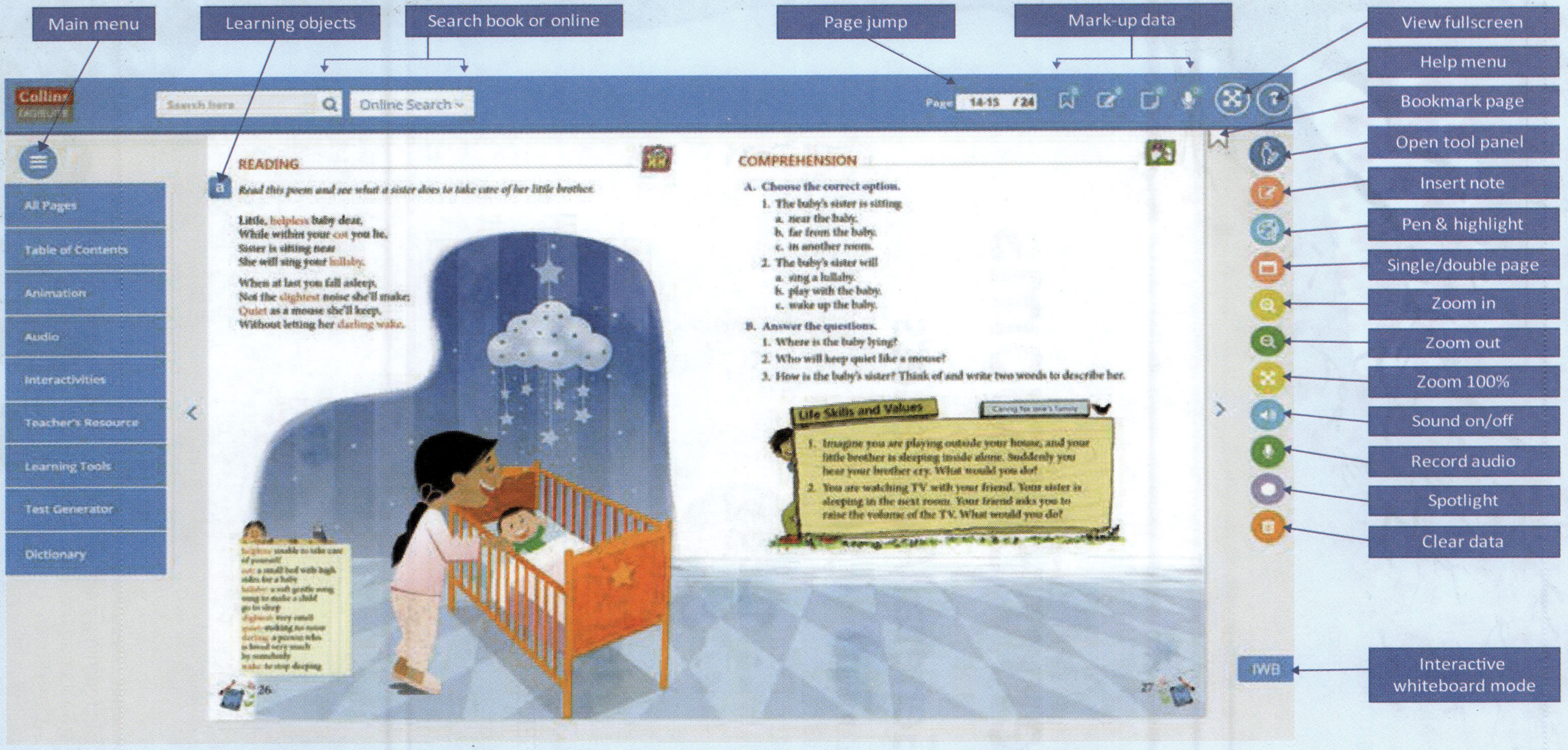

Student + Teacher			Teacher-only	
a animations	ia activities	g games	lp lesson plans	tn teacher's notes
ilt instructor-led tutorials	w worksheets	v videos	w worksheets	ak answer keys
	audio			

Preface

Cherry Blossoms provides graded, age-appropriate learning opportunities targeting holistic skill development for children in the age group of 3 years to 8 years. The series aligns with the vision outlined in the National Education Policy, 2020 for early years. It spreads across five levels, Nursery (Foundational Stage 1) to Class 2 (Foundational Stage 5). The books use a combination of hands-on activities, frequent recapitulation and child-friendly artwork to facilitate learning.

The series comprises **40 books** and spans **English**, **Maths**, **General Awareness**, and **Art and Craft**. The series comes bundled with a **workbook** for each subject and a book of **rhymes** and **stories** for Foundational Stage 1 to 3.

This series integrates the essence of **NIPUN Bharat** guidelines, which extensively deal with Foundational Literacy and Numeracy. The series aims to motivate learners to read independently, to improve their vocabulary, number sense and spatial understanding. The **Foundational Literacy and Numeracy (FLN)** skills include the skills for developing their critical thinking, logical reasoning and creative skills, as well as the skills to enhance their ability to express themselves both verbally and in writing.

Cherry Blossoms Teacher Support Materials include:

Teacher's Resource Books: Comprises stories, activity banks, classroom management and assessment guidelines

Multimedia eBook: Consists of animations, audio, video, slide shows, and interactive exercises

Print-ready Worksheets: Additional worksheets for practice and reinforcement, present in the digital support

Digital Flashcards: Flashcards with embedded sounds and animations for letter formation and letter-sound association

Animations and Songs: Animated stories and rhymes set to tune

Interactive Games: Interactivities to reinforce concepts in a fun and engaging manner

A note on the activity banks (included in the Teacher's Manuals)

The activity banks comprise hands-on activities that will help children develop the requisite skills to attain age-appropriate learning goals. In keeping with Howard Gardener's theory of multiple intelligences, the activity banks include options and variations that enable teachers to provide a planned cycle of experiences and opportunities, which foster each type of intelligence, to every child in their classrooms. The activity banks equip teachers to use the strengths of children as a means of complementing their less developed areas by valuing and nurturing the inherent abilities of the children.

Rani Thippavazzula, former Academic Director, Ravindra Bharathi Group is an eminent educationist with over two decades of experience in teaching, administration and curriculum design and development. As an Academic Advisor for chain schools pan India, she is proficient in developing learning products and is a specialist in Differentiated Instruction, Enterprise Education and Early Childhood Education.

Learning and Development During the Early Years

The early years are the most significant years for growth, development and learning. During this period, children need adequate opportunities for stimulating experiences as these favourably affect various learning abilities. Learning experiences, when chosen and planned properly, fuel the innate curiosity of children, and stimulate their thought processes.

The goal of learning during the early years is to enhance the all-round development of personality and to inculcate healthy attitudes, life skills and good values. Creative play, well thought-out games and developmentally appropriate activities help children develop the necessary skills to achieve these goals. The skills that children need to acquire can broadly be categorized as:

Motor:
Motor skills pertain not only to gross motor activities like walking and jumping but also include fine motor activities like the ability to hold a pencil and write. The development of motor skills is facilitated through several graded activities.

Personal, Social and Emotional:
Personal, social and emotional development, necessary for the overall personality development of children, is achieved using a combination of hands-on activities, role plays and thought-provoking stories and rhymes.

Linguistic:
The ability to listen, speak, read and write is critical to success in formal learning environments.

Mathematical:
The development of mathematical ideas and concepts is important at this stage since children will continue to build on this learning for most of their years of schooling.

Knowledge and Understanding of the World:
This is achieved through activities that enable children to explore their surroundings at home and in the school, and interact with the people that they see around them.

Health and Safety: The idea of health and safety is introduced through activities, stories and retelling of real-life experiences to encourage children to focus on health and well-being.

Creative:
Creative skills are developed through a host of activities involving art, craft, painting, roleplays, etc.

Logical and Rational Thinking:
Activities that involve simple puzzles, pattern-completion and visual discrimination help children to develop logical and rational thinking skills.

Contents

WALKTHROUGH

Short rhymes, set to tune, used to introduce fact-based concepts to facilitate recall. Follow-up practice exercises help reinforce the concept learnt.

Greetings

Sing.

When Mr Sun brings warmth and light,
When Mr Moon fades out of sight,
I say, Good morning everyone!

When the hands of the clock meet
on top of its head,
When Mr Sun makes me sweat,
I say, Good afternoon everyone!

When Mr Sun turns orange and red,
But Mr Moon is still in bed,
I say, Good evening everyone!

When Mr Moon is bright and white,
When Mr Sun is no longer in sight,
I say, Good night everyone!

Match the greeting to the situation.

Good morning! Good afternoon! Good evening! Good night!

Match the objects to their shadows.

Days of the Week

Sing.

Days of the week come and go
They never change, my mother says so.

Five days in a week to work and play,
Monday, Tuesday, Wednesday,
Thursday, and Friday.
On these days, I go to school,
I read a book, I splash in a pool.

Two days in a week to rest and play,
Saturday and Sunday.
On these days, at home I stay.
With my family, I talk and play.
When Monday comes back,
I go off to school with my bag.

Cross out (-) the things you don't do on Sunday.

Tick (✓) the things you do on five days in a week.

What do you like to do on Saturday and Sunday with your family? Draw in the box here.

Varied revision activity formats to ensure holistic skill development.

Revision activities such as these enable teachers to assess level of learning and recall without a formal assessment.

Rhymes and stories included to provide opportunities for activities and discussions that support social and emotional development.

Full-page illustrations to depict real-world situations. The use of complete sceneries enables teachers to go beyond the immediate concept and engage students in activities, discussions, etc. to explore a topic in more detail for enjoyable, discovery—based learning.

I Am Special!

Paste your picture in the box below.

Tick (✓) the letter your name starts with.

A B C D E F G H I J K L M

N O P Q R S T U V W X Y Z

Sing.

When I look into the mirror,
I see a smiling face looking at me.
It tells me I am special now,
Same as others but different somehow.

Look at the pictures. Listen to Ana's story.

This Is Me

Tick (✓) the correct box.

I am a ☐ | I am a ☐

girl

boy

Draw 3 things that make you happy.

Sing.

Turn around and see me.
This is me that you see.
I am friendly and helpful.
I go every day to school.

Turn around and see me.
This is me that you see.
I am kind and polite.
And I never fight.

Turn around and see me.
This is me that you see.
I love to dance and sing all day.
I like also to laugh and play.

My Body Parts

Point to each body part. Say its name.

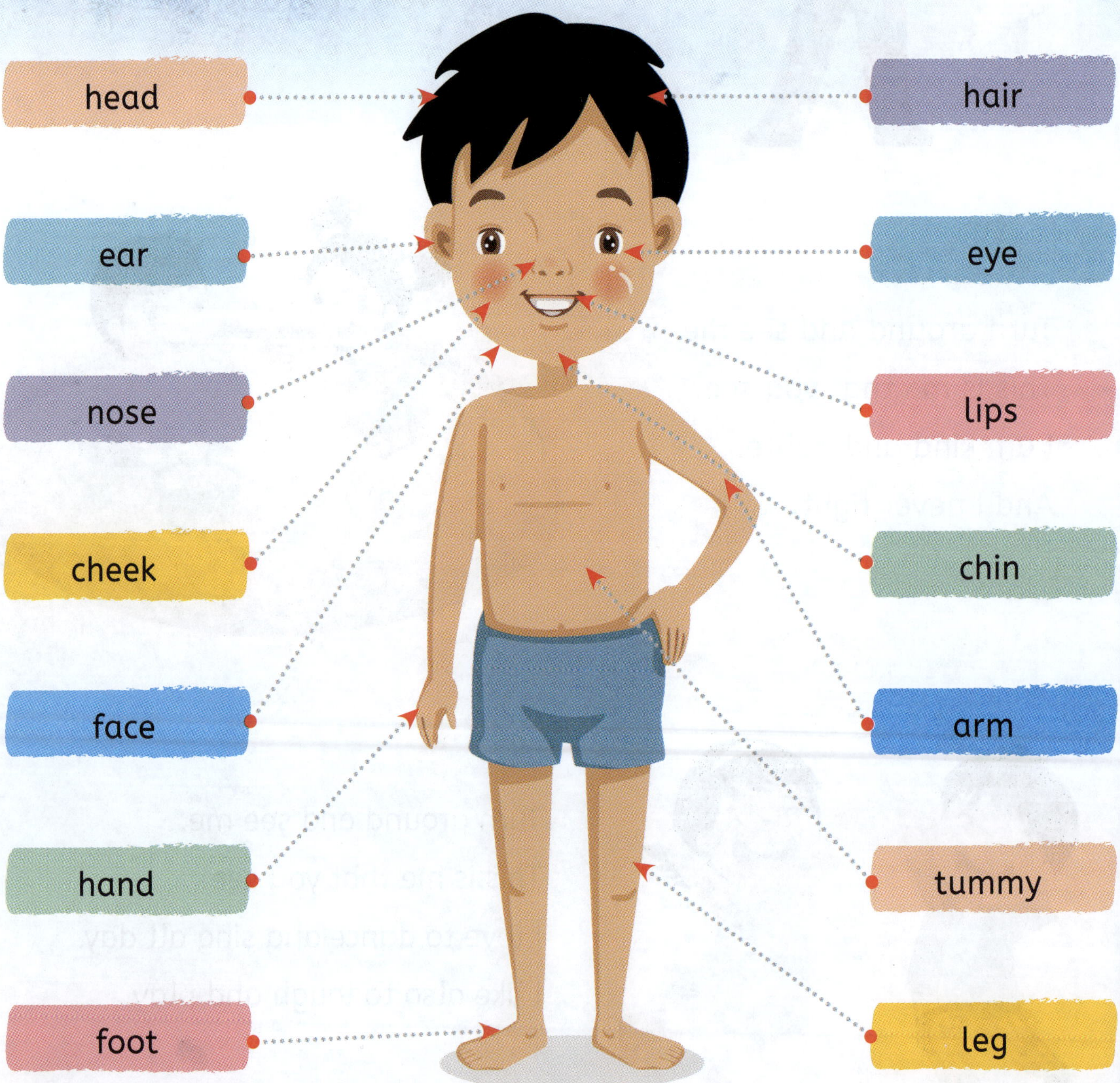

Look at the pictures. Draw one thing that you do with the given body parts.

hands

feet

lips

Keeping Clean

Look at the pictures. Describe what you see. Tick (✓) the things that you should do.

Sing.

Rini brushes her teeth every morning,
Rini brushes her teeth every night.

She puts paste on her brush,
She does not do it in a rush.

She brushes her teeth carefully,
She always cleans her teeth completely.

She rinses her mouth each time,
Bright, shining teeth make Rini smile.

Write the correct number next to each picture.

I Know!

Tick (✓) the correct option.

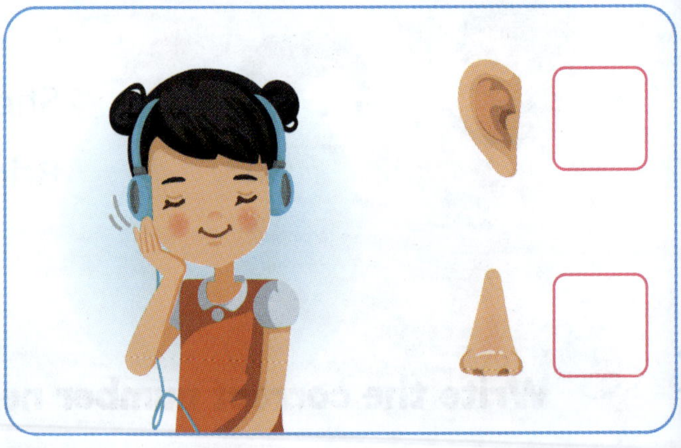

How do you get ready in the morning? Number the pictures.

This is My School

Join the dots to complete the picture of the school.
Colour the picture.

Tick (✓) the things you do in school.

Tick (✓) the things you see in your school.

My Classroom

Tick (✓) the things you see in your classroom.

Cross out (×) the things you should not do inside your classroom.

I Know!

Cross (×) the odd one out in each set.

Match the correct pictures to the school.

The name of my school begins with the letter ______________.

Match the pictures.

Fun Time

Spot 5 differences between the pictures.

Look at the pictures. Talk about what you see.

Listen to the story of three friends.

Greetings

Sing.

When Mr. Sun brings warmth and light,
When Mr. Moon fades out of sight,
I say, Good morning everyone!

When the hands of the clock meet
on top of its head,
When Mr. Sun makes me sweat,
I say, Good afternoon everyone!

When Mr. Sun turns orange and red,
But Mr. Moon is still in bed,
I say, Good evening everyone!

When Mr. Moon is bright and white,
When Mr. Sun is no longer in sight,
I say, Good night everyone!

Match the greeting to the situation.

Good morning!

Good afternoon!

Good evening!

Good night!

Match the objects to their shadows.

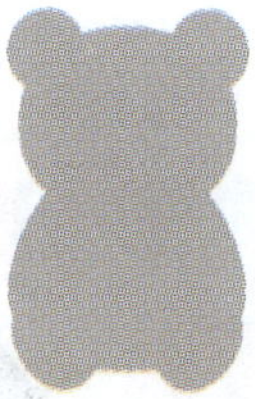

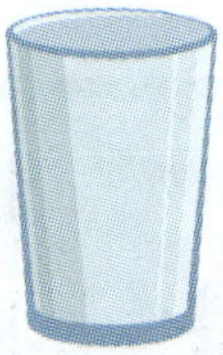

Manners

Look at these pictures. Tick (✓)the things that you should do.
Cross out (✗) the things that you should not do.

Paste the correct stickers.

Good choice	Bad choice

Emotions

Look at the pictures. Talk about what they show.

happy

sad

angry

surprised

tired

Look at these pictures. Tick (✓) the picture that tells how you feel.

My Family

Sing.

Come along! Come and see.
This is my family.
I love them, they love me.

When I cry, they make me smile.
When it is dark, they bring light.
This is my family.
I love them, they love me.

My family does everything for me.
I say thank you to them with a kiss.
This is my family.
I love them, they love me.

Draw the things you like to do with these family members.

Family Members

Touch the pictures. Say the names of the family members.

mother

father

baby

brother

sister

grandfather

grandmother

Paste a picture of yourself.

me

Ring the names of all people who live with you at home.

grandfather baby grandmother

father mother sister brother

Sing and enact.

Grandpa, grandma! Please don't go.
Grandpa, grandma! I love you so!
Grandpa, grandma! Please do stay.
Grandpa, grandma! Wipe my tears away.
Grandpa, grandma! I miss you so bad.
Grandpa, grandma! I really feel sad.

My House

Tick (✓) the kind of house you live in.

Draw a picture of your house.

Look at the pictures. Talk about them.
Name the objects you see.

living room

bathroom

kitchen

dining room

bedroom

Which room do you like the most? Why?

The Rooms in My House

Match the rooms in the house to the correct use.

Name the things you see in this room.

I Know!

Paste the correct stickers.

mother

brother

father

sister

grandmother

baby

grandfather

Tick (✓) the correct room that matches the action.

Means of Transport

Help the children reach school.

How do you go to school? Tick (✓) the correct answer.

Name these means of transport. Tick (✓) the ones that you have used.

I Know!

Match to the correct options.

Match the parts of the same picture.

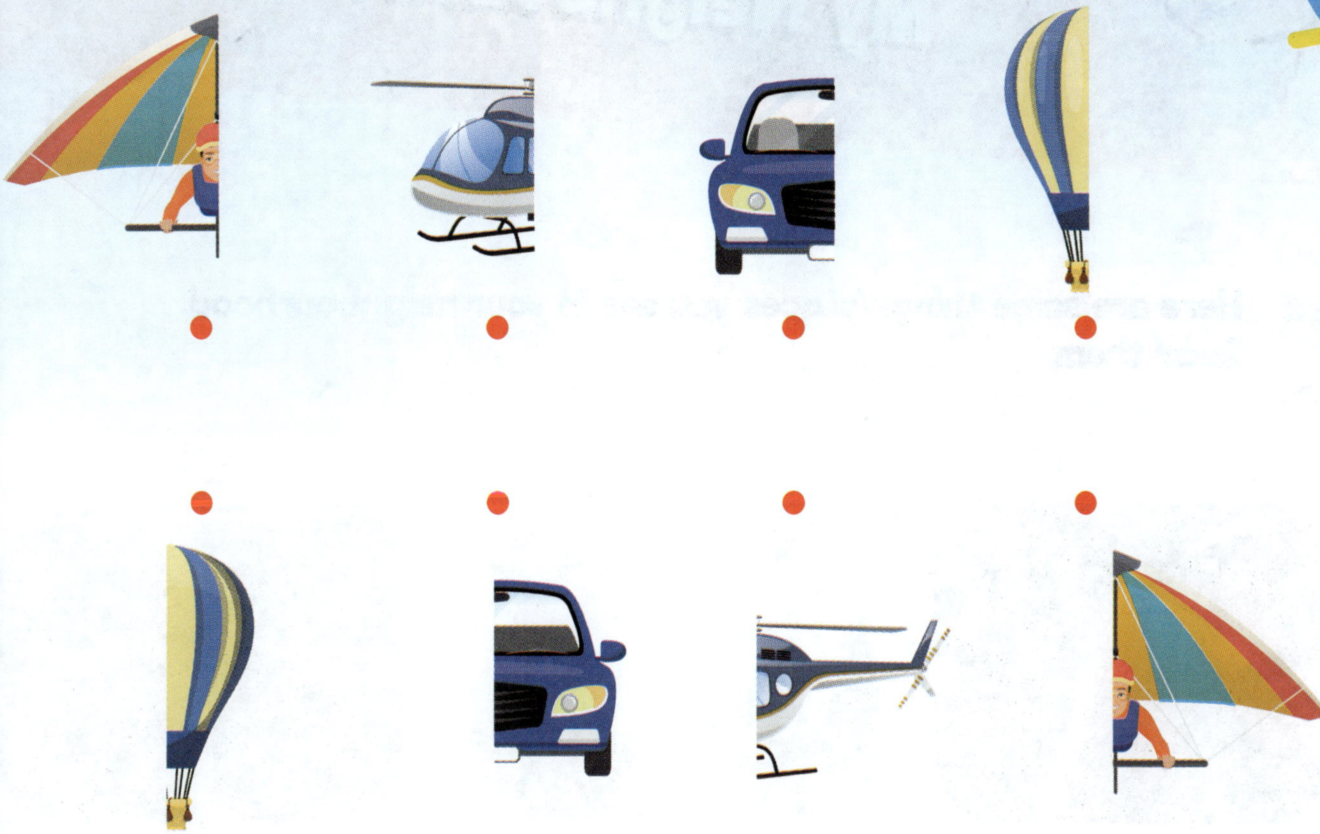

Cross (×) the odd one out.

My Neighbourhood

Here are some things/places you see in your neighbourhood. Read them.

market

park

road

garbage bin

bus stop

traffic

fire station

hospital

post office

Match the pictures.

People Who Help Us

Point and read.

doctor

grocer

policeman

cobbler

teacher

postman

nurse

ice-cream man

Use differently coloured crayons to take each person to their place of work.

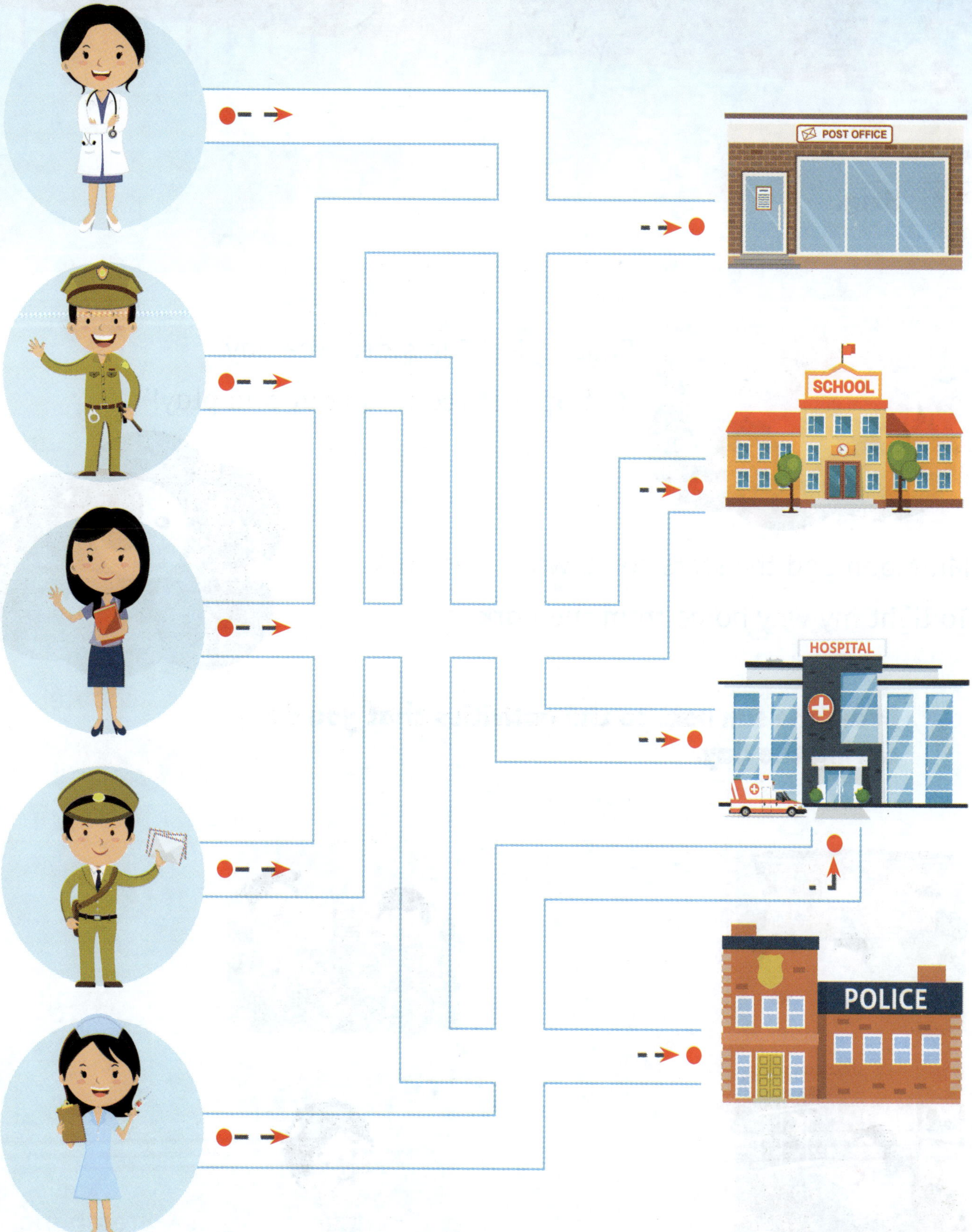

Day and Night

Sing.

Smiling Mr. Sun starts the day.
'Get up, get ready, go out and play!'

Mr. Moon and the stars come when it is dark,
To light my way home from the park.

Draw the sun next to the activities that you do during the day.

Complete the patterns.

Look at the pictures. Draw the sun and the moon to show night and day.

Days of the Week

Sing.

Days of the week come and go
They never change, my mother says so.

Five days in a week to work and play,
Monday, Tuesday, Wednesday,
Thursday, and Friday.
On these days, I go to school,
I read a book, I splash in a pool.

Two days in a week to rest and pray,
Saturday and Sunday.
On these days, at home I stay.
With my family, I talk and play.
When Monday comes back,
I go off to school with my bag.

Cross out (×) the things you don't do on Sunday.

Tick (✓) the things you do on five days in a week.

What do you like to do on Saturday and Sunday with your family? Draw in the box here.

Weather

Tick (✓) the things you see on the following days.

sunny day

cloudy day

rainy day

windy day

What kind of a day is it today? Tick (✓) the correct picture.

windy

sunny

cloudy

rainy

I Know!

Tick (✓) the correct picture.

Sun

Moon

Match the objects.

Paste the correct stickers.

Sunday

SUNDAY

Monday

MONDAY

Tuesday

TUESDAY

Wednesday

WEDNESDAY

Thursday

THURSDAY

Friday

FRIDAY

Saturday

SATURDAY

Hello Colour Red

Point and read.

engine

fire vehicle

fire station

post office

Colour the watermelon red.

Tick (✓) the objects that are red.

Hello Colour Yellow

Point and read.

sun

sunflower

ice cream

banana

lemon

smiley

school van

cheese

yellow crayon

Find all the things that are yellow. Circle them.

Hello Colour Blue

Colour the sky and water blue.

Complete the patterns. Use the correct colours.

Use blue colour and okra to paint the whale in the water.

Hello Colour Green

Colour the globe blue and green.

Teacher's Note: Point out the Indian subcontinent. This is a good opportunity to introduce the idea that the Earth is our home. It is made of land and water. We should keep the Earth clean.

Hello Colour Black

Point and read.

black cat	black crayon	bat	crow	ant

Colour the leopard. Print with cotton buds to show its spots.

Paste stickers of objects in the night.

Hello Colour White

Point and read.

cotton

clouds

white hare

snow flakes

Paste cotton on the sheep.

Paste strips of paper on the old man's beard.

I Know!

Tear and paste black and white paper.

Match the ball with the correct bucket.

Colour the image in the given colours.

Fruits

Touch the pictures. Say the names of the fruits.

apple

mango

papaya

banana

watermelon

orange

strawberry

grapes

pomegranate

Take the fruits to the bowl.

Vegetables

Touch the pictures. Say the names of the vegetables.

okra

onion

pumpkin

cauliflower

potato

broccoli

carrot

cabbage

Draw and colour 3 vegetables that you like.

Flowers

Touch the pictures. Say the names of the flowers.

rose

lotus

lily

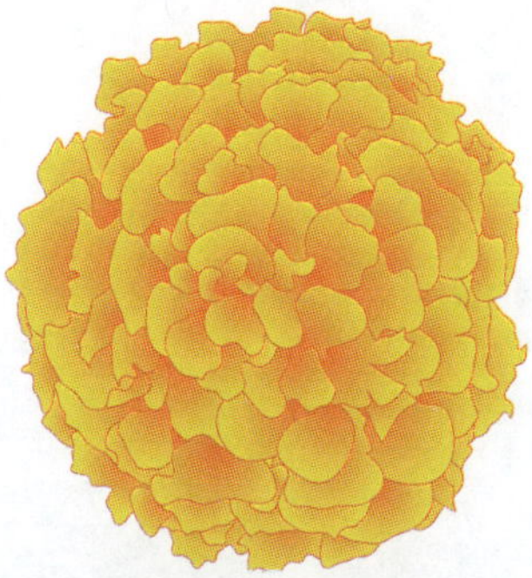

marigold

jasmine

sunflower

Match the flowers to their shadows.

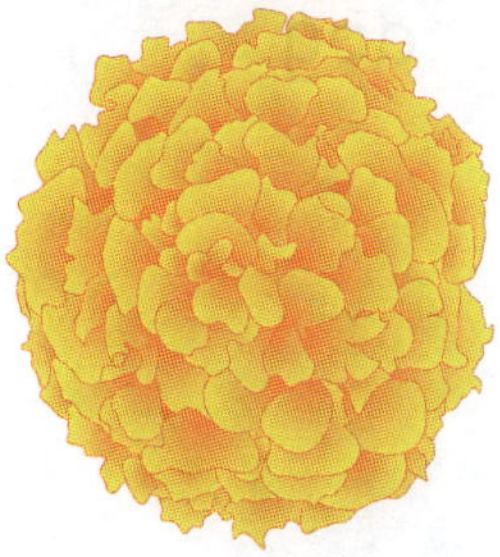

Animals at Home

Touch the pictures. Say the names of the animals.

cat

dog

fish

hamster

rabbit

birds

Join the dots and colour the picture.

Match the animals to their tails.

Animals on the Farm

Touch the pictures. Say the names of the animals.

duck
cow

Animals in the Jungle

Touch the pictures.
Say the names of the animals.

Write P for pet animals. Write F for farm animals. Write J for the animals in the jungle.

I Know!

Colour the same fruits with same colour.

Lead the baby to its mother.

Cross (×) the odd one out.

Identify the vegetables. Cross (×) them out.

Caring for Animals

Look at these pictures. Talk about them.

Look at these pictures. Cross out (✗) the pictures that show things we should not do.

Fun time

Sing the tic-tac-toe song. Play with your friends.

Tic-tac-toe song

Tic-tac-toe, around I go.
If I miss, I take this.

Teacher's Note: A group of 3-4 children can play this game. The children take turns to place their finger on the starting position. Ask everyone to sing the song while the player traces a circle on the page. The player has to answer the question their finger lands on.

Sticker page

Page 29:

Page 40:

Page 57:

TUESDAY

FRIDAY

MONDAY

SATURDAY

Page 67: